MW00772628

The Pirelli Calendar

Universe

Design: Damiano Viscardi

Translation: Studio Queens

Cover: Dawn Bossman, Elizabeth Smith

First published in the United States of America in 2001
by UNIVERSE PUBLISHING
A Division of Rizzoli International Publications, Inc.
300 Park Avenue South
New York, NY 10010

2001 2002 2003 2004 2005 / 10 9 8 7 6 5 4 3 2 1

Printed and bound in Italy

Library of Congress Control Number: 2001094246
ISBN 0-7893-0658-1

Contents

Introduction

It all started in the Sixties. The English Sixties, when rock was starting to become all the rage, when swinging London was the groovy place to be for lovers of visual arts—photography and movies.

Derek Forsythe was no exception. A bright young Londoner, well acquainted with trendy photographers, he landed his first job in the marketing department of the English Pirelli after finishing his studies. The post did not really seem to fit the photographer's creative urge, which had little in common with the needs of an industrial group, which produced and marketed tires. But in those years of transition such an odd mix was bound to produce surprising results. It worked out for the young Londoner, who was lucky to work for a company "enlightened" enough to sense his hidden potential. So when in the middle of 1963, after just a year in the company, he told his boss about an idea of his, he found no closed doors. The idea was actually welcomed. It was, in fact, a tempting concept. The year before, a pin up calendar was published aimed at tire centers: why not replace it with the sophisticated work of a brilliant talent from London's miscellaneous world of visual arts? The subject was a classic theme: female beauty. Forsythe's boss at the English branch thought about it for a minute and, after briefly calling Milan, okayed the proposal. The young marketing man flew to the Balearic Islands with photographer Robert Freeman. Two weeks later, the twelve photographs of the 1964 calendar were ready to go to press. The Pirelli calendar was born.

At the time, art productions of all sorts were plentiful, and the calendar probably went relatively unnoticed in its first year, unsupported by the media launches and

promotional events later introduced. But over the next two years, the calendar, with its simple and liberal pictures, was already bearing precious witness to contemporary times. People were talking about it. Some of the few copies printed were mailed to glamorous addresses such as John Lennon's place and Buckingham Palace, where the calendar was sent to Prince Philip of Edinburgh.

So when in 1967 the calendar was not published—for reasons unknown to history and unrecorded by company files—many people noticed its absence. And many made themselves heard: complaints got so intense that in 1968 the special issue came out again, followed the next year by a version of the calendar which is to be remembered among the most daring ones thanks to the images "captured" by Harry Peccinotti on the West Coast, a venue much celebrated by major movies and books published in those years, from *Blood and Strawberries* to *Zabriskie Point*. The calendar thus confirmed its function as a reliable witness to the hectic post-1968 years. This role was reinforced in the following years, when the calendar was entrusted to the best photographers of this cultural *milieu*, from Sarah Moon—the first woman to get an assignment, and the first person to show a naked breast—to Hans Feurer, who broke a long phase of creative inactivity with the calendar.

The 1974 calendar marked the passing of a decade and coincided with much changed times, from the creative drive of the Beatles to the sinister years of terrorism. Those were dark times, worsened by the oil crisis and the many uncertainties of a world suddenly confronted with the problems of much-contested resolution. Those were not calendar years and in 1975 the Pirelli one ceased to be print-

ed. In its absence it remained the object of discussion, an indication of the new climate and an impossible presence in the restless years of such a profound crisis.

A decade was to pass before it reappeared in 1984 when the conditions were right for its rebirth. It was produced by the British Pirelli once again, which brought in a new art director. Martin Walsh was a middle-aged gentleman resident in Switzerland where he lived off the earnings from the many ads invented as a leading creative force in one of the world's major advertising agencies. From 1984 on the Pirelli calendar became his principal task and he produced a display of ideas without precedent. The 1987 calendar presented black women for the first time with a slightly immature sixteen-year-old, unknown to the fashion catwalks, a certain Naomi Campbell; the Olympics calendar came in 1989, a very non-olympic year; the ballet calendar (1988) featured an anomalous male presence. One of the factors that made the gift increasingly special was the introduction of the tire tread theme in the form of a discreet sign, hidden in the photos. It was like a hidden mention, similar to Alfred Hitchcock's habit of appearing in one frame of his films, with the spectator having to identify him. The same applied to the Pirelli tread marks that were turned into jewels (1987), fabric patterns (1985) and decorative banners (1992).

The Martin Walsh era continued for approximately a decade. Then Pirelli decided to bring the art direction of its calendar into the company. This was in the early Nineties and it had just come through a major crisis marked by a reorganization that jolted it from top to bottom. The Milan Company was then ready for a relaunch. This also affected the calendar which set off in 1994 along a new path under the guidance of the communications management of the group's leading company, which entrusted its creation to the best photographers—from Richard

Avedon to Peter Lindbergh, Annie Liebovitz, Herb Ritts and Mario Testino and Bruce Weber, all the great names of photography went through the 'Cal' experience as it had now become known in English slang. The photographers may have been protagonists but so were the models, chosen not from the famous names of the catwalks but from those who had yet to make it—from a very young Kate Moss (1994) and Christie Turlington (1995) to Laetitia Casta, the star of the 1999 calendar photographed by Bruce Weber and the 2000 one by Annie Liebovitz. With this formula the calendar established itself as a cult object of the end of the millennium. It was an object of desire that everyone wanted and hardly anyone had. The world press started to talk about months in advance, trying to gain information on the set to pass on to its readers. In the meantime—further proof of its now recognized artistic value—the photographs started an international tour that has taken them to the world's leading museums: from Palazzo Grassi in Venice to the Carrousel du Louvre in Paris and the MASP in Sao Paolo. This itinerant exhibition designed by Gae Aulenti has visited ten countries on three continents and is about to arrive in Japan. Who knows whether, on that day in 1963, the enlightened manager who approved the project of his young employee with a passion for photography could ever have imagined all this...

Pirelli 2001 Calendar

photographed by Mario Testino

2001 – JANUARY

2001 – AUGUST

2001 – SEPTEMBER

2001 – OCTOBER

The Pirelli Calendar 1964–2000

1964
Robert Freeman

There was no grand launch,
no public relations effort,
and no response from the
newspapers.
What did happen, though,
was that Pirelli began
to get letters from dealers;
for some reason Pirelli, after
the calendar, was suddenly
popular.

MICHAEL PYE, *THE PIRELLI CALENDAR ALBUM*, 1988

1964 – FEBRUARY

1964 – MARCH

1964 – APRIL

1964 – MAY

1964 – JULY

1964 – AUGUST

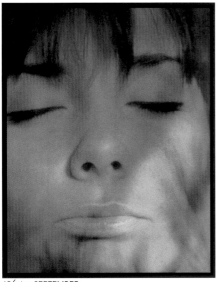

1964 – SEPTEMBER

1964 – OCTOBER

1964 – NOVEMBER

1964 – DECEMBER

1965
Brian Duffy

The 1965 Calendar presents
an image of a girl who is the
symbol of a new era.
A beautiful girl dressed in
the same way as her
contemporaries, the same
as many that could be seen
in those times in the streets
of Paris, London or Milan,
sitting at a table in a café and
smoking. A girl alone, a girl
who would look a man in the
eyes and assess him before
choosing.

GIAMPIERO MUGHINI, *PANORAMA*, JANUARY, 24TH, 1997

1965 – FEBRUARY

1965 – MARCH

1965 – MAY

1965 – JUNE

1965 – JULY

1965 – AUGUST

1965 – SEPTEMBER

1965 – OCTOBER

1965 – NOVEMBER

1965 – DECEMBER

1966
Peter Knapp

1966 – JANUARY

1966 – FEBRUARY

"What we did in the calendar was already the limit of what you could do then and the models were careful."

PETER KNAPP

1966 – MARCH

1966 – APRIL

1966 – MAY

1966 – JUNE

1966 – AUGUST

1966 — SEPTEMBER

1966 — OCTOBER

1966 — DECEMBER

1968
Harri Peccinotti

1968 – JANUARY

It is an open question
whether many read poems,
but they were piled high
in basement bookstores...
The calendar team found
poems about love...
and found girls to match
the words...

MICHAEL PYE, *THE PIRELLI CALENDAR ALBUM*, 1988

1968 – MARCH

1968 – APRIL

1968 – FEBRUARY

1968 – MAY

1968 – JUNE

1968 – JULY

1968 – AUGUST

1968 – SEPTEMBER

1968 – OCTOBER

1968 – NOVEMBER

1968 – DECEMBER

1969
Harri Peccinotti

1969 – JANUARY

1969 – FEBRUARY

"Everywhere you turned on the beach there were incredible looking girls, just very sexy girls and they were doing whatever they felt like... I said we wouldn't have to take models or anything; we'd just go and photograph people having a good time in the sun."

HARRI PECCINOTTI

1969 – MARCH

1969 – APRIL

1969 – MAY/COVER

1969 – JUNE

1969 – JULY

1969 – AUGUST

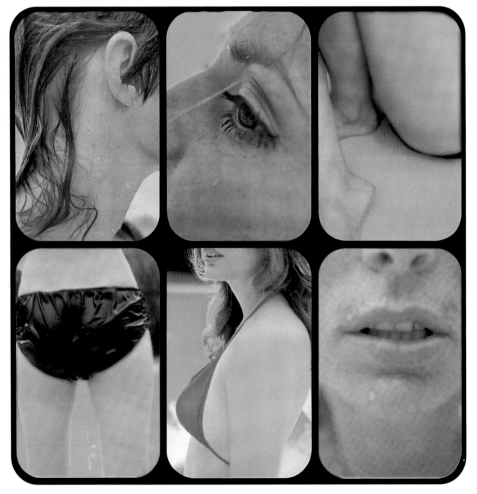

1969 — SEPTEMBER

1969 – OCTOBER

1969 – NOVEMBER

1969 – DECEMBER

1970
Francis Giacobetti

Giacobetti always planned
to dramatize sea and sky,
sometimes setting a tiny girl
against a tumult of clouds
and a sparkle of water;
everything was shot on a
very wide angle lens, and
through special filters which
he had devised.

MICHAEL PYE, *PIRELLI CLASSICS*, 1994

1970 – JANUARY

1970 – FEBRUARY

1970 – MARCH

1970 – APRIL

1970 – MAY

1970 – AUGUST

1970 – JULY

1970 – SEPTEMBER

1970 – OCTOBER

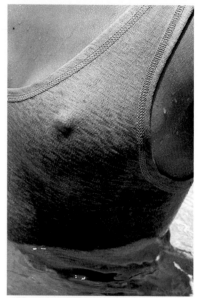

1970 – NOVEMBER

1970 – DECEMBER

1970

1971 Francis Giacobetti

In the 1971 calendar...
Giacobetti pursued the
romantic soft-focus,
moonlit tones; here and
there some garage mechanic
probably felt shortchanged,
given the screaming nudity
offered by the "specialist"
press. By this time the
advertising message of the
calendar was canvassing the
four-thousand-odd lucky
recipients..., not to mention
those not on the list who
tried to procure it through
auction.

GUIDO VERGANI, *THE PIRELLI CALENDAR 1964–1998*, 1998

1971 – JANUARY

1972
Sarah Moon

In an impressionist climate, lenses reveal a pair of naked breasts for the first time.

SÉRGIO BEREZOVSKY, *VIP*, SEPTEMBER 1997

1972 – COVER

1972 – JANUARY

1972 – FEBRUARY

1972 – MARCH

1972 – APRIL

1972 – MAY

1972 – JUNE

1972 — JULY

1972 — AUGUST

1972 — SEPTEMBER

1972 — OCTOBER

1972 — DECEMBER

1973
Allen Jones

But it was clothing that
caused a furore in 1973. Pop
painter Allen Jones clad the
models in fetish gear. Parts
of the prints were airbrushed
in imitation of these paintings,
so that real faces and bodies
marged into fictional ones;
the women became
imprisoned in the illusions.

SARAH KENT, *TIME OUT*, MARCH, 26TH, 1997

1973 – JANUARY

1973 – FEBRUARY

1973 – MARCH

1973 – APRIL

1973 – MAY

1973 – JUNE

1973 – JULY

1973 – AUGUST

1973 – SEPTEMBER

1973 – OCTOBER

1973 – NOVEMBER

1973 – DECEMBER

1974
Hans Feurer

1974 – JANUARY

1974 – FEBRUARY

1974 – MARCH

1974 – APRIL

1974 – MAY

1974 – JUNE

1974 – JULY

1974 – AUGUST

1974 – SEPTEMBER

1974 – OCTOBER

1974 – NOVEMBER

1974 – DECEMBER

There'll be an empty space
in the boardroom wall
next year: after ten years
of imposing stylish sex,
Pirelli have decided to stop
production of the most
prestigious calendar.

COLIN DUNNE, *DAILY MIRROR*, MARCH, 28TH, 1974

1984
Uwe Ommer

The symbol of swinging
London's best years
returns—triumphant as
a ship in a victorious fleet,
as warm as the South Sea
sands, as sensual as a
Polynesian tamuré—it's the
Pirelli calendar.

STEFANO ARCHETTI, *L'EUROPEO*, NOVEMBER, 26TH, 1983

1984 – COVER

1984 – JANUARY

1984 – FEBRUARY

1984 – MARCH

1984 – APRIL

1984 – MAY

1984 – JUNE

1984 – JULY

1984 – AUGUST

1984 – SEPTEMBER

1984 – OCTOBER

1984 – NOVEMBER

1984 – DECEMBER

1985
Norman Parkinson

Now, some time later, after
having scrutinized the two
Riace bronze statues from all
angles and concluded that
there was nothing more
beautiful than the male form,
I confess I've changed my
mind because there's really
nothing more beautiful than
live women, some being
even more beautiful in
photographs; in fact, they are
perfect only in photographs.

GIORGIO SOAVI, *EPOCA*, SUPPLEMENT, DECEMBER 1984

1985 – APRIL

1985 – MARCH

1985 – MAY

1985 – JUNE

1985 – JULY

1985 – AUGUST

1985 – SEPTEMBER

1985 – NOVEMBER

1985 – DECEMBER

1986
Bert Stern

"Removing the Sense of
Guilt From Nudity"—the title
of the June photograph in
the Pirelli calendar—
summarizes the philosophy
of the entire project.
Not that much guilt is still
attached to nudity. If a barrier
of modesty has fallen with
the 1986 calendar, it does not
concern the nudes but the
photographs, which, for
the first time (and without
any sense of guilt), claim
their share of the attention.

ROBERTO DI CARO, *L'ESPRESSO*, NOVEMBER, 24TH, 1985

1986 – COVER

1986 – JANUARY

1986 – FEBRUARY

1986 – MARCH

1986 – APRIL

1986 – MAY

1986 – JUNE

1986 – JULY

1986 – AUGUST

1986 – SEPTEMBER

1986 – OCTOBER

1986 – NOVEMBER

1986 – DECEMBER

1987
Terence Donovan

There is always a moment (which the photographer can summarize and reconstruct almost theatrically), during which a glance, a gesture, an expression, can elicit a reaction, a desire, or a dream.

ITALO ZANNIER, *THE PIRELLI CALENDAR 1964–1998*, 1998

1987 – COVER

1987 – JANUARY

1987 – FEBRUARY

1987 – MARCH

1987 – APRIL

1987 – MAY

1987 – JUNE

1987 – JULY

1987 — SEPTEMBER

1987 — OCTOBER

1987 — NOVEMBER

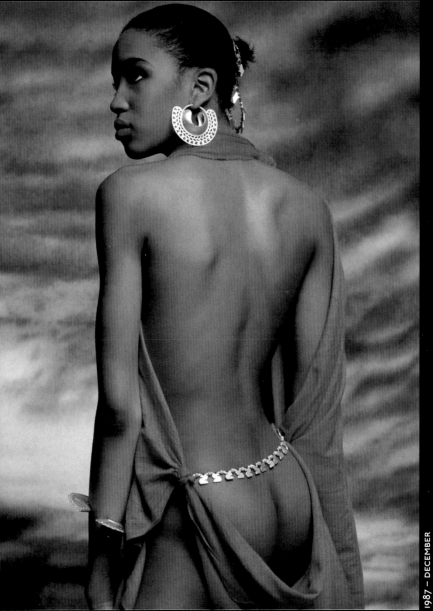

1988
Barry Lategan

All it took to secure the 1988 calendar a place in history was that idea of the man's silhouette, that sort of spiderman with a tiretread stamped on him.

GUIDO VERGANI, *LA REPUBBLICA*, NOVEMBER, 7TH, 1987

1988 – COVER

1988 – JANUARY

1988 – FEBRUARY

1988 – MARCH

1988 – APRIL

1988 – MAY

1988 – JUNE

1988 – JULY

1988 – AUGUST

1988 – SEPTEMBER

1988 – OCTOBER

1988 – NOVEMBER

1988 – DECEMBER

1989
Joyce Tenneson

1989 – JANUARY

1989 – FEBRUARY

"I love this camera, and I love the way it manages to reproduce skin tones."

JOYCE TENNESON

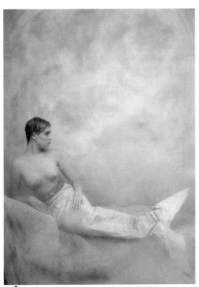

1989 – MARCH

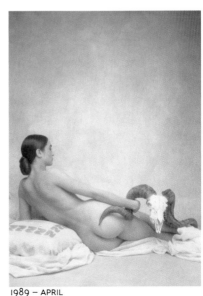

1989 – APRIL

1989 – MAY

1989 – JUNE

1989 – JULY

1989 – AUGUST

1989 – SEPTEMBER

1989 – OCTOBER

1989 – NOVEMBER

1989 – DECEMBER

1990
Arthur Elgort

When in 1990 Arthur Elgort photographs
women in the style of Leni Riefenstahl,
these pseudo-Olympic athletes must wear
at least a short skirt with the tread marks.

PETER DITTMAR, *DIE WELT*, FEBRUARY, 5TH, 1997

1990 – COVER

1990 – JANUARY

1990 – FEBRUARY

1990 – MARCH

1990 – APRIL

1990 – JUNE

1990 – JULY

1990 – AUGUST

1990 – SEPTEMBER

1990 – OCTOBER

1990 – NOVEMBER

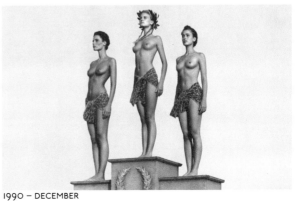

1990 – DECEMBER

1991
Clive Arrowsmith

Undress for history, please

THE EUROPEAN, NOVEMBER, 9ᵀᴴ, 1990

1991 – COVER

1991 – JANUARY

1991 – FEBRUARY

1991 — MARCH

1991 — APRIL

1991 — MAY

1991 — JUNE

1991 – SEPTEMBER

1991 – OCTOBER

1991 – NOVEMBER

1991 – DECEMBER

1992
Clive Arrowsmith

Dragon-women, monkey-women, tiger-women, horse-women. The Pirelli calendar springs out of an exciting cocktail blending mysterious China with female charm, following English photographer Clive Arrowsmith's idea.

MASSIMO DI FORTI, *IL MESSAGGERO*, NOVEMBER, 12TH, 1991

1992 – JANUARY

1992 – FEBRUARY

1992 — MARCH

1992 — APRIL

1992 — MAY

1992 — JUNE

1992 – JULY

1992 – AUGUST

1992 – OCTOBER

1992 – NOVEMBER

1992 – DECEMBER

1992 – SEPTEMBER

1993
John Claridge

These nudes, with all the pornographic nudity that is available, are almost a return to the Garden of Eden.

GILLO DORFLES, *CORRIERE DELLA SERA*, NOVEMBER, 15TH, 1992

1993 – COVER

1993 – JANUARY

1993 – FEBRUARY

1993 – MARCH

1993 – APRIL

1993 – MAY

1993 – JUNE

1993 – JULY

1993 – AUGUST

1993 – SEPTEMBER

1993 – OCTOBER

1994
Herb Ritts

Four of the world's top supermodels,
the photographer behind Michael Jackson's videos, Madonna's fashion stylist, Kim Basinger's make-up artist, Michelle Pfeiffer's hairdresser... on a deserted beach in the Bahamas.

SUE WILLIAMS, *THE WEEKLY*, NOVEMBER, 25TH, 1993

1994 – COVER

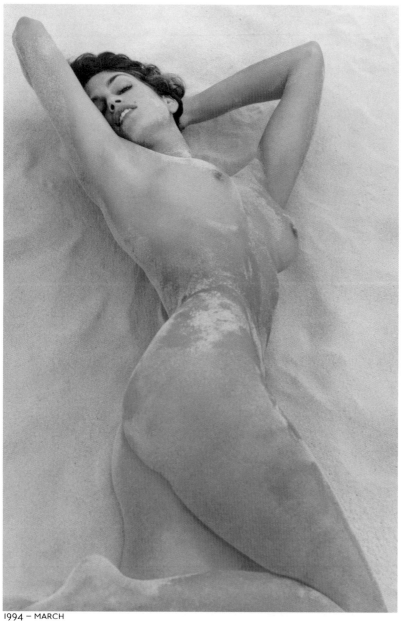

1994 – AUGUST

1994 – JANUARY

1994 – FEBRUARY

1994 – APRIL

1994 – MAY

1994 – JUNE

1994 – SEPTEMBER

1994 – JULY

1994 – OCTOBER

1994 – NOVEMBER

1994 – DECEMBER

1995
Richard Avedon

Richard Avedon 1995 calendar is the real classic, full of fantasy and a vivid reminder that, before he became quite so grand as he now is, he was the very best fashion photographer going.

JOHN RUSSELL TAYLOR, *THE TIMES*, FEBRUARY, 7TH, 1997

1995 – JANUARY

1995 – FEBRUARY

1995 — MARCH

1995 – APRIL

1995 – MAY

1995 – AUGUST

1995 – SEPTEMBER

1995 – OCTOBER 1995 – NOVEMBER

1996
Peter Lindbergh

"Nothing is sexier than personality. The woman that has the courage to be herself is automatically sexy, even without high heels and a miniskirt."

PETER LINDBERGH

1996 – FEBRUARY

1996 – MARCH

1996 – APRIL

1996 – JUNE

1996 — MAY

1996 – JULY

1996 – AUGUST

1996 – SEPTEMBER

1996 – OCTOBER

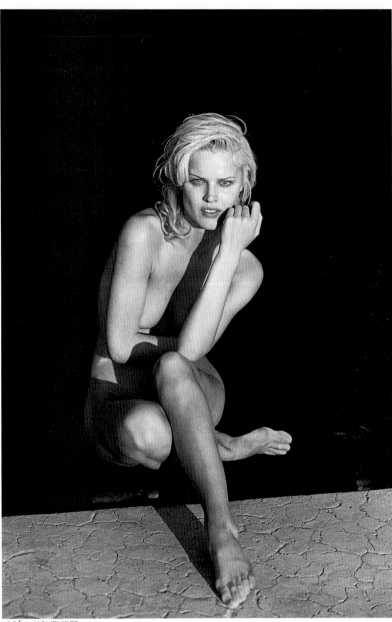

1996 – DECEMBER

1997
Richard Avedon

If the original calendar was a product of 1960s notions of liberated sexuality, its current incarnation is in step with the multiculturalism of the '90s.

CAROL SQUIERS, *PHOTO*, MARCH–APRIL 1997

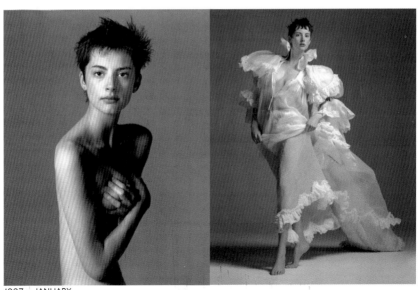

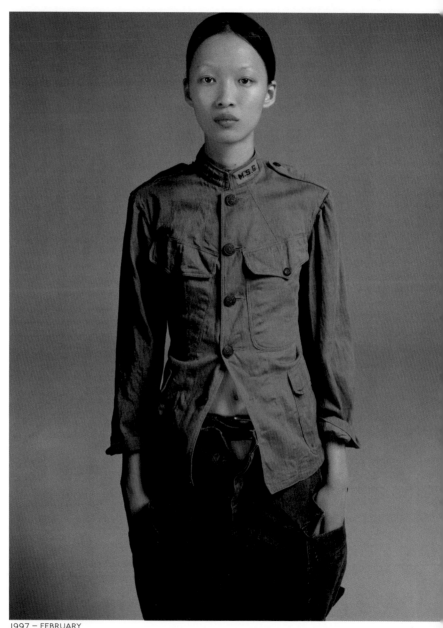

1997 – FEBRUARY

1997 – MARCH

1997 – APRIL

1997 – MAY

1997 – JUNE

1997 — JULY

1997 – AUGUST

1997 – SEPTEMBER

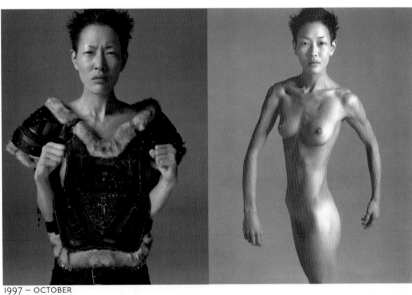

1997 – OCTOBER

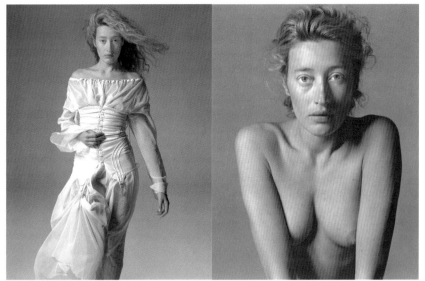

1997 – NOVEMBER

1997 – DECEMBER

1998
Bruce Weber

For the 25th-anniversary edition, Weber broke with tradition and included photos of famous (clad) men alongside the usual drop-dead (not so clad) babes. His title: "Women that men live for, Men that women live for."

SUE ZESIGER, *FORTUNE*, JANUARY, 16TH, 1998

1998 – COVER

1998 – JANUARY

1998 – FEBRUARY

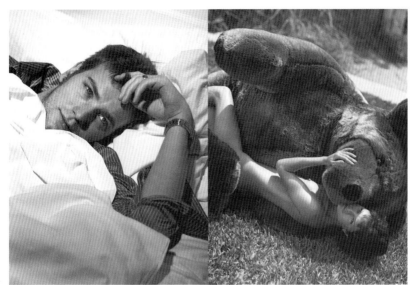

1998 – MARCH

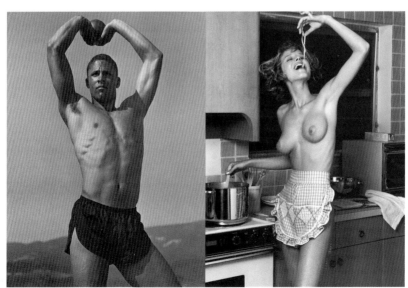

1998 – APRIL

1998 — MAY

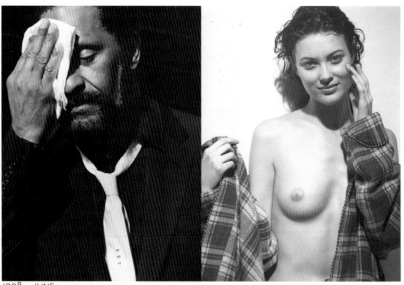

1998 — JUNE

1998 – JULY

1998 – AUGUST

1998 – SEPTEMBER

1998 – NOVEMBER

1998 – DECEMBER

1998 – COVER

1999
Herb Ritts

London gets its new Pirelli every November... at the same time that Paris gets its Beaujolais... The 1999 calendar by Herb Ritts is a retrospective of all the great female myths of the 1900s.

SOPHIE CARQUAIN, *LE FIGARO*, NOVEMBER, 23RD, 1998

1999 – JANUARY

1999 – FEBRUARY

1999 – MARCH

1999 – APRIL

1999 – MAY

1999 — JUNE

1999 – JULY

1999 – AUGUST

1999 – SEPTEMBER

1999 – OCTOBER

1999 – NOVEMBER

2000
Annie Leibovitz

"I am a big admirer of very
classic work. When Pirelli
asked me to do the calendar,
it was an opportunity for me
to work out this exercise of
looking at women in a very
classic way. This is really
like joining a club... a very
exclusive club. I was also
very excited about the idea
of being a woman and being
asked to do the Pirelli
Calendar."

ANNIE LEIBOVITZ

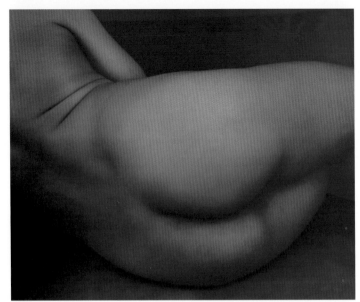

2000 — FEBRUARY

2000 — MARCH

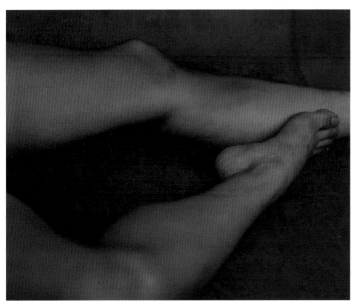

2000 – APRIL

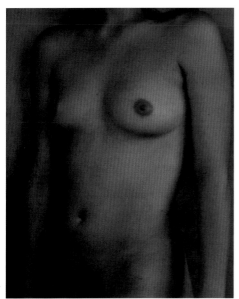

2000 – MAY

2000 – JUNE

2000 – JULY

2000 – AUGUST

2000 – SEPTEMBER

2000 – OCTOBER

2000 — NOVEMBER

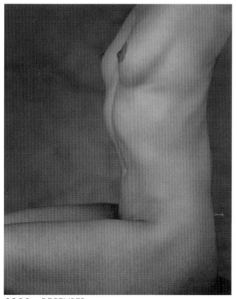

2000 — DECEMBER